Avant Garde Poetry Chapbook

Gael Sweeney

ISBN: 978-0-578-02670-1

Avant Garde Poetry Chapbook

Gael Sweeney

Struggling Artist

She is an artist, an art contender
Her brush paints despite despair and gender
Pencils heed letters from the sender
Kindhearted acts from the creative heart
Artists, remembered for creating smart
She is an artist, a life defender.

She pretends her work will be remembered
Pastels scuffing the page with bristle,
As they touch a gleaming magic crystal
Ceramic vases linger quaintly above
Brushstrokes brawl amidst her submissive glove
She is an artist, peaceful pretender

She understands she doesn't have the answers
She says you should look at things verily
Pens dance about the page quite narrowly
Artists aim to change the precarious world
Paints aspire not to be quickly hurled
She is an artist, now gone asunder

Saint Lover

A lover like an angel whacks out his remark
How dar'st cross my path, you female philosopher
On a long journey I am about to embark
The journey of blessed Saint Lover of hereafter
This could not be true of a fiery, hot dancer.
Of this Irish god whom I've longed and awaited,
Not this could be true of my intelligent seer,
Now I know my fears will not be abated
Thou art the wondrous realm of fantasy princes
Therefore, my dreams have all been in vain to prevail
You thought the garlic healed me with my life of
defenses
Yet, you would never lift your dense, masculine veil
But now he says he's leaving me eternally
Me thinks this is the end of graceful sanity.

Golden Dawn

Fruitful delights of dawn arise,
Whereby justice reigns upon a new day,
Moher's Cliffs of daisies shall fantasize
Of gods yesteryear who wolf cyclic hay.
If not, the fairies returned to the caverns
Where they hibernated amidst dirt trolls
And made love among the fiery dragons
Winter thrusted ice upon primal coals
It was a place immersed in living blood
Bog kings and queens alike struck red solstice
Lamastide waters flowed, birthing a flood
Irish immigrants abandoned the homestead,
Secrets washed away in the dingy mud
A voice cried from the green Irish terrain
Me forefathers who scream welcome again.

Flowing Freely

Jolly sunlight glows upon a writer's rose.

It knows well cheerful days and starry nights,

Burning desires and songs it would compose

Otherwise, it takes honorable flight

Into the realm of fairies bathed in springs

Where little does the rose expect to find

Submerged sea kings immersed in anchor rings.

Flowers were only hoping to unwind

To share seashell kings' joyful dance with glee

But an author decides it be maligned

Tossed into the yester-year debris,

Two minds who were poetically entwined

In authentic writers fraternity

Now Flow freely in Eternity

Benevolous Existence

May Gaelic Waves bring benevolous peace,

As Air is She with whom you have the fling,

Earth gives you the duplicitous release

And the sky dips you into the hot spring.

Gael Waves hit rocks piled upon an alms dish

Of grass fields with emerald greenery.

Sky's beloved horse fought with the chosen fish

Bringing peace to you by green scenery.

May spiraling Waves bring peace resplendent

May Air return Sister Sun her Earth-Wheel

And essential Earth remain transcendent

While existential Sky reaps the surreal.

Be death's demeanor not duplicitous

Be life's journey simply benevolous.

Snow Purifies Rain

I'm sitting, having morning coffee,
Which I've stopped drinking for the most part,
And trying to write a poem about rain,
Watching it turn to virginal-pearl snow,
Thinking of changing this warm, heartfelt poem
About long-lost, pure flakes,
Trying to make my existential thoughts
Less abstract so you now understand them.
The last time it snowed was the day of burial.
Grandpa's coffin was laid beneath the oak,
And I often think of him, far away.

In cold north-lands, beneath earth's white gown,
Lay the best companion a child's ever known.
Snow flutters through the traffic-laden streets,
I sit alone with my coffee blackness
Red lights flickering into green eyelids,
Thinking about what means the free life
Circular orbs, formed by baptismal snowballs
I see blue spots reflected on water
Whilst the heavy sky clashes down on land
And people continue on their journeys
Into the wide, solitary spaces

The last time it snowed was the day of burial
Grandpa had gone away for good this time
More than a decade ago,
He was buried in this snow.

Snow plummets on dirt bathed in bright sunlight
The baptism she always awaited.
Earth rises and meets cottony white clouds
If only the rocks would complete her,
She who bears joy about broad white spaces
Wishing only to be consumed by light
Hanging upon the moonlight of black night
In which the Raven penetrates what's right
Never knowing when to go into flight
Hoping that her wings are closed very tight
Otherwise light might journey further in
To the chambers of her inner night

Sacredness of Nature

Snow melts and reveals underlying spices
Soon spring divulges delicate foresight
Shadows fall within shallow crevices
And sunshine shows mysteries to delight
Oh! Where did the past go this last decade?
Weren't you the wise one who counted
shamrocks?

Was it all really a masquerade?
Along mystic shores at noon each day
When I thought my life would pass slowly
But that was when I embraced youthfulness
Everything participated wholly
In the sacredness of nature's truth.
Today, it seems the elements combine
In the right place: air, breath and the divine
Are one hundred years old and first inspired,
Yet, earth is many times her age, thinking,
Rocks should have infiltrated through sinking.
Sinking, sinking, and never again blinking.
Where he will find delightful indulgence
Amidst her growing, pulsing white sunlight.
One hundred years old when first devoted,

Yet, earth was only twice her age, thinking,
Rocks should have infiltrated though sinking.
Yet, sinking, sinking, never again blinking.

Photos of Ireland

Italian Poem 1

Che' guardi a me, spirito solo,

Non sai che ho un altro sapore,

E non conosci il tuo ruolo,

Spirito, non capisci mio amore,

Dio mio, sei uno spirito libero,

Che segue la cantatrice d' opera

In un romanzo quasi come un sogno

Finisci con te che adopera giuochi

Tutt'i' trucchi tuoi della maschera

Sono sempre mia,

incluso e' l'arte di fare la Madonna,

E poi, ci sono tempi quando sembro una donna vipera,

L'unica sono io, la primadonna

Se tu potessi capire solo che

Ti amero' veramente sempre

Seriamente col cuore.

She Possesses Fair Glow

Amorous, all that the sunlight does to night
She possesses fair glow and golden glare
Her eyes are stony globes in moonlight
I would not let her take me anywhere.
Her precious shine is not fresh and youthful
She is an ancient whirlpool that eats friendship.
Nor would I say she is strictly truthful
Else, she would end your celestial kinship
But most of all, what gently ignites me,
After all she forged upon the terrain,
Is light glowing up there eternally?
Bestowing the Moon with dreamer's disdain
If love lingers to taste longevity,
Lament lovers longing her mystery.

Love and Life Force

One questions the meaning of eternity
From early childhood to late in one's life
Pondering, is there one reality?
A question that creates a lot of strife

And even when one comes of golden age
The heart beats with a fluttery rhythm
For fear of being caught naked offstage
In a symphonic beat polyrhythm

Much like the heart in blue anxiety
But lingering happily with actors
Building timeless notoriety
In the name of one's drama detractors

How dare one take the path that is carefree?
Love and life force interacting in thee.

Alone

It's always this way on Saturday,
Look at this earth that,
Divides us,
The love that you freely give to me,
Look at liberty,
Separation,
Soon it will be for eternity,
Eternally one
And the same.
Never see one another again
Yet, always one
Together
In this great, dreamy Universe
I will wait for you
Your return
When the elements fuse into one
The heart will beat there
In Creation.

Ancient Subliminals

Loving fills her veins with delight tonight
After all, the willows sway in the winds
Water beats rock-hard in the twilight
And the moon tastes delights of the highlands

Fog obscures winding paths to delight
While branches scratch through misty, black velvet
Her heart seems to engage in dewy flight
Over the rays of traveling regret

Often such heavenly events occur
Mist meets men merrily celebrating
Ancient events like when Pompeians were
In the wine cellars of Bacchus—waiting

But if you don't mind meeting
my ancient subliminal needs
Then universe will manifest great deeds

Touching Her Heart

Meek, gray skies infringe upon her silence
Storms pound on Pandora who waits alone
Only she dares touch a box in defiance
Nor does she wish to have a chaperone

For now, she says all the princes must go
And they cannot touch her body-heart zone
Some might think she complains of woman's woe
But there are her skills she wishes to hone

Clouds drop from the skies to workers' heartlands
Pandora, with a hard hat, picks up the phone
The universe, she replies, makes demands
That she will now dance to his saxophone

When it comes to love, it's joyous glee
For she finally exchanges vows verily

St. Brighid's Well, Ireland

The Irish Well

Early, you heard terrestrial pitter-patters
Moving onward
In airstreams of poetry
Time kissed your poems
Oblivious to reason
As intuition held the answer
Cutting forcefully into core heart values.

Why not take a walk across the cityscape
Into fields of your ancestors
Where you'll find a lovely daisy that shines
Upon the barriers of an Irish well?
The same daisy your granddad saw
As he was about to embark for lands afar
It burst into little pieces – white, green, and yellow.

A golden moonbeam christened its crown
As the beam looked back into darkness,
Ringlets expanded themselves
From Brighid's well invoking rebirth
They spread in dense, velvety waters
Luke warm, embracing nude limbs
Of the maiden who emerged.

In your mind's,
Perpetually penetrating apparition,
Light burst, and your heart danced
Alas, arose earth
Later, you received celestial blessings
From gentle winds of poetry,
And lyrical waves.

Swimming

Immersed in limpid waters,
You are Poseidon,
Creator of pleasure
Arms pushing in outward motion,
Legs, kicking up and down
Till you reach eternal tunnels
Of spiraling waters
Gushing backward
As your body shoots forth in a burst
Flying upward from ocean to sky
Sirens wish they could embrace you
But you're on another plane.

A black mountain
Hides an orange sunset
Sneaking over its edges
With rays embracing you
Much like chains
Poseiden discovers the all-encompassing nature
of four elements:
Earth, wind, air and water

Mermaids enclose him.

He has swum twenty laps

Across the pool

Amidst the health club

Encircled by New York's skyscrapers.

Three Graces stare at his muscular body

Much like the oak tree with ogham inscriptions

Letters of ancient times

Written from top to bottom

Hawthorne and oak

Which tree are you?

Graces dance with arms reaching upward

Legs moving back and forth

Across the wooded land

Now they're exotic dancers

But they're not potent enough to distract you

Power gushes downward

Across your face and body

The mud from Mount Etna

The blood from the Parthenon.

As Poseiden moves forward
From black mountain to waters, he dives
Back to his place of origin
With schools of fish
Starbursts in the hearts and minds of men.

Poseidon takes his place alongside the
Mythological gods and goddesses
All knowing to set a good example
All accepting of the difficult journey
Anticipating Odysseus' return to Penelope
Starstruck because he is in you,
A bursting explosion of artistic empowerment
In unison.

Shattered Silence

Serendipity saw séances sincerely supposing
She saw ships travelling seaward so . . .

Shells shattered suddenly in sifted sand
Sun shined supposing shallow sadness
Shook and shattered her sallow silence.

By the way, beaus bore boring betrothals
Before boys bought buoyant balloons
Beaming and bouncing beyond the beach

Betrothed beaus in my brothers' barn
Banned the boys' bicycles
Because they thought the thistle
Might inadvertently thrash their silence.

Purity

Crystal clear nuptials extend purity
Froth like silken wholesomeness resigns
Nature brings forth golden-haired charity
Environmental structure's sole designs

Such views are part of universal truth
When the lilacs plant their roots below
Raindrops fall lyrically on the roof
Puncturing green pathways through rose fellows

All one must do is seek intuitive reasons
Rainbows sought by all those leprechauns hold gold
Nature brings forth all the righteous seasons
But an answer to loneliness cannot hold

Wisdom rests in the philosophers' books
Packed at the Irish National Library
To give novices better outlooks

On My Shoulder

Sun setting upon my shoulder,
Overbearing clouds roll in my nostrils
I breathe out cool, mist
In a green field, my body extends
Corn arises from my navel
Fashioned dolls of husks and vines
The grape leaves entwined
My feet press upon the fruit
Which arises through my toes
At once
A man I am
Fading away with Mother Earth
Her dirt intermingling my essence
Sparkling in gold and silver
An Impressionist picture
Entering the witchy world
From rocks to Gaels
Blessed songs of Barleycorn from woods
Brethren betrothed before bewildered
Bystanders beneath earth and Barley
Bystanders brew grain before bemusement
A bewildering beginning
Bringing forth life

Why I Went to Ireland

Last summer, I travelled to Killarney,
One of my stops in starry Ireland
The Irishmen believe they hold the Key
After touching Blarney stone with their
hands

At first we stopped in lands emerald green
Just as we've heard in fairy stories told
It was the most spiritual place I'd seen
For fancy whispers its ancestors hold

Not to mention the abandoned rock farms
Homes gutted across the desolate lanes
And walls of endless stones seem like
ghosts' arms
No longer do they have mom's window
panes

The reason I traveled there was to see
Everything the immigrants had told to me

Always a Poet

Always a poet who dares not confess

That the moon cannot read his duress

Now his honest, lyrical thoughts suppress

That he invokes utmost women's fondness

There's no chance he will ever adore me

Because I am only one who admires

An ephemeral artist who loves to be free

Although to be like him my heart aspires

Always a poet, whilst he dare not sway

Day and night, night and day, of him I think

Knowing those moons that love him, meet
dismay

When pain prevails, I'll just commit a whim

My spirit and earth revolve around him

If only I were a young girl again

Love is You at Breakfast Time

Love is your bright smile at breakfast time
A warm cup filled to the brim of goodness
Joyful moments spent not costing a dime
Toying with all your dreamer's finesse
With brown eyes and flowing ringlet curls
You shyly hide a few locks of gray
Upon a white cloth embroidered with pearls
You gave to me with intent to portray
All the love, and coffee sips overjoyed
That led your immense worldly thoughts astray
Over the years, we have truly enjoyed
Those brown sugar bags in creamy café
A brown waterfall cascades in a mug
The steam arises with honey into the jug

Ireland

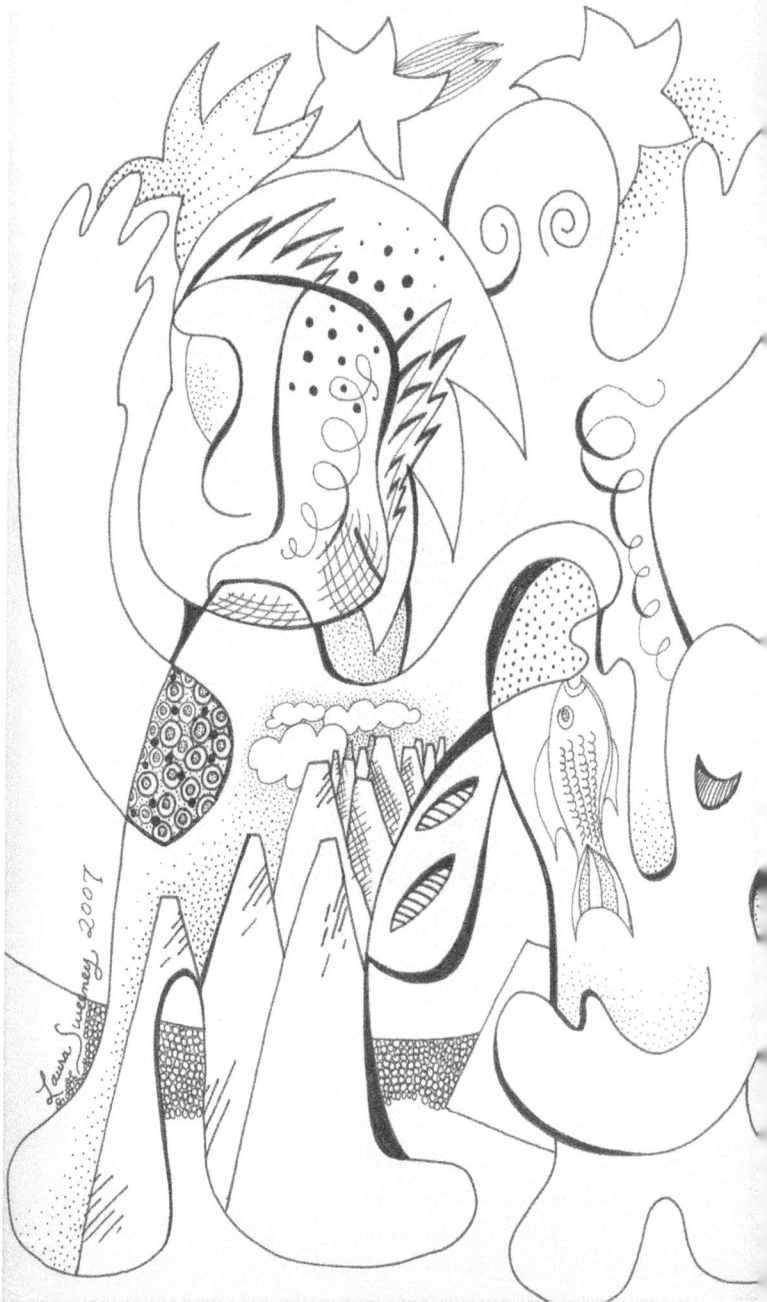

Carmen

Looking back . . .
Little Carmen pitter patters in the pathway
The little one carries a bounteous bouquet
Sings in the garden where sun rays pass through tree tops
Where little swamp fairies skittle-scuttle nonstop
Across gardens hang magnificent garlands
Above lily pads floating in this rosy dreamland
Carmen dreams of times years ago.
When she played with her mom who did not outgrow
All those little things that to girls pertain
Occupations entertaining from which girls sustain
All their hopes and dreams of castles in the fog
With knights who offer their hands to ignite Yule logs

Gaia

Like a stream of espresso,
Her hair flows from the mountain top
In undulating curls
That descend down hillsides
Belonging to ancient
Trees and trolls, as she is Goddess Gaia
Filling the green slopes and rocky cliffs
With bountiful springtime delights.

Among the hungry peaks
Await husky rock huts all hollow and hallowed
By tourists who come here to explore family heralds
Their coats of arms with knights' helmets upon them.
Goddess Gaia is Goddess of the night
Their morning tea and graceful Irish delight.
The one who brings fresh floral growth.

New beginnings emerge from behind rock walls
As she brings forth stars
And her body arises from black dirt
Reclining on the earth, surrounded by grape vines
And children with fruits of their labors
Seeds open in fields where sunflowers shine like suns
Say hello to sunny days and sallow shiny shields

Emerging, Emergent Soul

The soul pressing from earth emerges tall
As the spirit happily seeks fulfillment
Green-eyed psyche next door deviates all

But the green soul seeks through art to enthrall
Because it does not reach diminishment
The soul pressing from earth emerges tall

Your inner mind wishes to have a brawl
As if it possessed some type of ailment
Green-eyed psyche next door deviates all

Your pink heart says it would like to install
Emergent hopes, desires in atonement
The soul pressing from the earth emerges tall

The human race should evolve after all
And seek to become all benevolent
Green-eyed psyche next door deviates all

Emerging, emergent remains in recall
Notwithstanding mankind's discouragement
The soul pressing from the earth emerges tall
Green-eyed psyche next door deviates all.

POETRY

Poetry
Word pictures?
Inspired, meditative?
Enticing, teasing, evoking
Love and conflict, Aggression and Playfulness
Flowing, dancing, emerging
Rhythmical, graceful
Lyricism

Falling

Ascending

Diminishing

Increasing

Eternal

Shared, reflective moments that unite spirits
playing parts.

Starry Knight

The knight's far and I await his return.
I will wait for him despite fleeting time.
His absence provides me worldly concern.

He knows not what it's like when all saints yearn
But I will wait for the divine sublime.
The knight's far and I await his return.

Has he once considered that he must earn
stars that gently evoke internal rhyme?
His absence provides me with worldly concern.

Greeks enjoyed showing heroes on their urns.
Mine is in my mind where upward he climbs
The knight's far and I await his return.

Now I can say I once loved to adjourn
Outings into the hillsides at nighttime.
His absence provides me worldly concern.

I know he has reached the green water-fern
And has consumed salty, yellow-green lime.
Was it the food of gods in a Greek urn?
Ambrosia and nectar grant his return.

Children Learning

Children run through the halls of sensory learning
Not knowing where their nursery books will take them
Too soon nowadays, they're decisively adjourning

To television's arms exploring their yearning
For inappropriate views rather than sublime
Great books by authors who are discerning

Freestyle

I love the freestyle poem
That emerges with sunrise each day,
The one that's about to burst forth
As Endurance and display
As Fortitude taking form
Creativity the norm.

It's exploration of evocative symbols
Repeatedly impressing the writer,
The reader, too,
In a manner to heal and to deal
With obstacles so real
Barriers—irrational, and surreal.

Freestyle form gives meaning to our zeal,
Not faithfully following rules of order,
But there isn't a major disorder
To defeat poetry's free-flowing recorder
And if rhythmical lines were freestyle,
Free-flowing love could be worthwhile.

.

Hurt Feelings

Feelings that get to the tippity-top
Like a hallowed hole on heavy hearts
A dive into the deep sea sponge mop
All gooey because feelings have no smarts
I feel radiating pangs that spread out
Leaving emptiness in the inner core
Suff'ring means so much that I'd thrash about
While weeping, wishing I'd suffer no more
This seems to be the result of long life
In which I can never be satisfied
Spasms of a racing heart breathing strife
Always presuming breath's disqualified
If vision were bright and love were free
Maybe hurt feelings would understand me

A Portrait of Joy

Joy visits all people and loves giving
A sweet feeling after an embrace
Touching your smooth, fair skin to show caring
When you make a painting with splattered white
And textures that vary across the board
Hoping your love will be in your sight
When you write poems to give him rewards
Joy's having children run across the yard
And a smooth, blushing red kiss on the cheek
Daffodils blooming to adorn get well cards
Because you hurt him without thinking last week
Joy's when we heal after the mental storms.
It's making up and bringing forth new art forms.

Joy 2

A feeling of breathing in a rainbow
Of diverse hues that warm a happy heart
And living life simply without falsity
So everything felt flows freely outward
For eternity, forgetting woes
And being heard by someone who listens
Not minding that earth's terrain ages
Now that the moon is the timeless sage
When sunlight bursts forth from my florid chest
One with nature, and doing its very best
Loveable lullaby bursts into universe
Rhythm's head gently rests on one of many books
Caressing music with warm tender looks.
Thus, joy awaits.

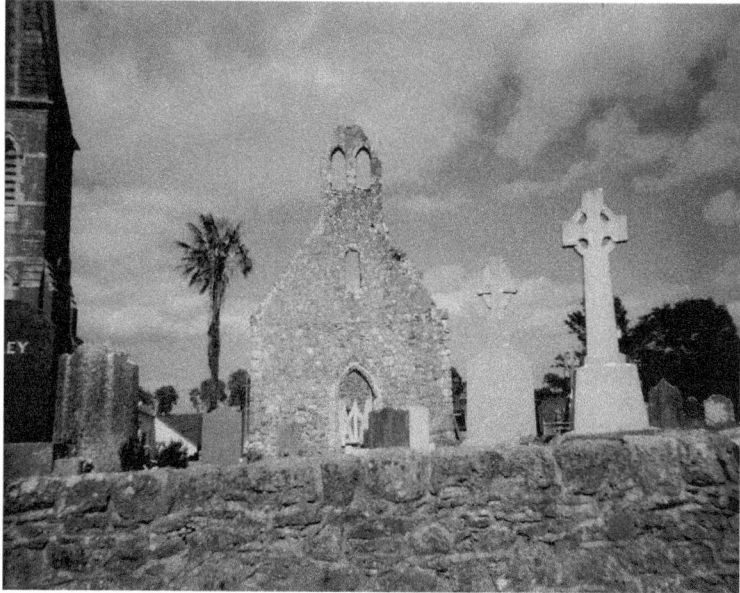

What If We Were a Sestina?

Saintly poem to be made into us

Few rare days remain along our journey

Conflicts brought us along pathways and pastures

Into rolling riversides, rich with red

Leaves smelling like stale acorns along birch

Trees reaching their branches to bare breasts

At last, we play nude along this journey

And there's nothing we can say as pastures

Embody navels that give seedlings bright-red

Plantlets that mimic the odor of smooth birch

Along your trunk, I will hide my oak chest

As it is purely a poem to embrace you

For this is just a journey along pastures

When the end of the day strikes sunset-red

Smelling the fresh scent of ivory birch

Remembrances of our mothers' sweet smiles

When crossing's end comes to gently greet us

Back in cradles of heavenly journeys

Upon birth, a blue-baby first sees bright red

And feels something rough like rare, rotund birch

A silly mouth signals its mother's breasts

None other than the poem that is us

A persistent, perpetual journey

That one days ends in bucolic pastures

Your trunk resembles a sturdy, bright birch

Strong enough to resist branches on breasts

Winds of change terrestrially touch you

But are merely dream images of journeys

No big deal as we both turn to pastures

Having experienced flowing sun-red

Is your favorite color still rosy red?

Your spirit reminds me of fondling birch

A hand moves across your chest but skips my chest

An ethereal poem enraptures you

The sound waves along a joyous journey

As we join forefathers in green pastures

Yellow, blue, green, purple, orange and red

Paint like a rainbow across the fair birch

Poetic circles that resemble birth

A Couplet or Trio?

Our sunlight stole the couplet from Italy
This is the best thing it ever did with glee
How would grass survive the long hours in Moonlight
Without a soul to give it some reciprocal insight?

The big dipper is old now and not so chic anymore
Her starlight decided she had become a bore
With the light's gray-streaked tresses and falling skin
Never would the Moon touch the dipper's body again

Instead, he found a pretty bell of the ball
Upon whose tresses Moonlight immediately did fall
No longer could he see the dipper had become a Sage
And that the best of wisdom does come with age

Not how you look that counts when it comes to love
But, rather, how sincerely you give your heart above
Sure, it's great to be radiant and pretty
To have all the gold to make them happy

But next time you decide to steal someone's glee
Remember just what happened to sunlight
For when you hurt others by stealing their love
Your heart shall feel pain from Heavens above

Honest Sonnets Trio, and a Couplet
•

Honesty presides in these fresh sonnets
Where breathing seeks to set example
For future generations on thresholds
Of honest wit staying apt and ample
Poets questioning meanings of long life
While judging and pretending honesty
They hold themselves above impending strife
And espouse flamboyant ideas' majesty
Honesty leads the art of poetry
For a poem swallows up the reader
Engulfing him with eternal bardolatry
Wise words breathe an eternal breeder
If poets just stopped phony contrasting
Perhaps poems would live everlasting
♫

How does a new poem live forever?
Let me count the ways poems purify
Through female free-form and virile villanelle
If only they knew to demystify
Poetry who writes to catch attention
He did not get from his early childhood
A quiet child worthy of mention
Whose poems represented brotherhood
Reactions of interconnectedness reign
Sultry sounds stream to entice sentiments
A hope that senses will linger the same
That baby poems do dance like Bacchants
That the earth-bard could only smash thoughts through
So his poem would dance dreamily inside you.

♫

From the heart blooms colorful rose bouquets,
Surrounded, a sweet seizure flutters upright
In gushing, garrulous melodic phrase
Made to fit undying spiritual rite
Hearts merge and hands do as saints' souls
entreat
Fragments of stained glass rest in chapel's
skylight
Form and message merge on rustic countryseats
Bucolic grazing land's tearful twilight
Poetry overwhelms overt outcasts
On journeys into the poet's caves
A mysterious abyss of absinthe
Pathways crossing upward to vivid waves
Where, at last, souls meet to exchange nepenthe
That simply symbolizes completeness
In every illustrious, starry sweetness
♫

Poetry is breath
To us bequeath!

Playful Sestina

My poetry is not as fine as Sestina's
Hers consists of memorable terms
And is completely down to grounded delight
Whereas mine rests in coarse cliché' lines
Her poems are masked in ancestors
Pillars of suave society that play

No doubt, I can believe Sestina's wise terms
She has shown that she understands delight
And her head is not up in the cold lines
Sestina is dedicated to her ancestors
Everyone knows her for her widespread play
No doubt, the heartfelt heavens will be hers

Thank goodness ones like you are loving delight
That everyone's minds are not in the terms
Loners without affable ancestors
People like me who incite play
That becomes golden dreams to inflame your
Judgment of Sestina's musical words

You pulled me down from whence I hung in
terms
Within white wings of angel's ancestors
But never did you see my savant play
Timid treasures remarkably like yours
From now on, you must heed my wary words
We are two beings grounded in delight

Besides, everyone loves Sestina's ancestors
Whose pictures she immortalizes in play
Perhaps, I would like to celebrate yours
If not with art, then within astute terms
Like Sestina did with lyrical delight
Taking me on a trip through lively lines

Don't forget that which said your ancestors
That you should utilize poems for play
And that the treasures of hope never stray

Reading to Heights

Discovery isn't the evidence
Real red leaves float in a clean, careful
coincidence
From the tall trees in front of her Victorian home
Speckling the green grass and lawn
A child extends across the lawn
A book in hand
Colorful photos spark interest in worlds afar
"One day I'll travel far and wide," she says,
Leaning her head on her palm
Sighing
Birds chirp a light melody

If only she were a bird
With wings to fly far-off
Into the spacious sapphire yonder

Like a fairy princess,
She would grow wings
Take off in escape
From the green, spotty monster with the long
arms
Who has attacked the heroin in her romance?
Along comes a puppy with eager eyes
A cool breeze dries sweat dripping down her
forehead
Another sunny afternoon on the lawn
Could be many a girl
Developing artist or researcher
Red lipstick pressed into a locket
Gooey feeling as she rubs her index finger across
The shiny foil on page five
Possibly the knight's shield
Stained with blusher
Maybe he'll be the one who'll dash her off her
feet

Middle-aged Woman

She needs to develop her mind,
Moreover, the inner ideas shine whilst the body
sags

Arms of rugged muscle from hard labor
Two children now grown, beautiful stars
But remains the middle-aged woman
a protagonist
In a world that values youth, not wisdom?

She was once known as Aphrodite
Goddess who emerged from the foamy waters
Into a starry mist

Imagery

Flickering sunlight springs
Needs pierce angelic lungs
Hope lovingly breathes

The Demon Pollen
Penetrates open column
Oh! A gasp of air!

If only You do
Return your beam joyously
And give my lungs breath

Life is an enduring lesson.

Sweet Vanilla Evokes Memories

She didn't know to put it on the shelf

Where sweet, vanilla evoked memories

And lilacs bloomed beside the window

Now had come the truth that she expected

A Lark and a Nightingale foreshadowed

Her cunning artist hid authentic secrets

In shallow streams shown across sheets

Of his diary, and ink-blot drop drawings.

Another meal, another ritual

When they sat but never spoke any words

Just another question mark on her face

Staring and wondering the true meaning

When would he leave for his eternal flight?

Water evaporating in their pot

Of rice suggested love's epiphany.

Reminiscences Suggest Eve

Returned reminiscences really crushed him

He now knew not to put them nicely away

Where wisdom with wonder wiped out memories

And lilacs lie upon Eve's lace garden quilt

Now, no one had known the newness of Adam's love,

but

An owl whistled, "woo-hoo," while the woman's
whereabouts

Where unknown to the handsome hero who hurried her

Through shallow streams shown in his drawing book

His diary was designed with ink-blot drawings.

No more meals, or righteous rituals, he thought.

The two sat, but they never took communion

Quandaries and question marks on his face

Staring and starting to be startled

When would he wear wings for his flight to find her?

Where had she gone this fine evening?

"Meow," sounded their kitten.

"Hiss," sounded the snake from the garden.

Then he knew where she'd have gone
To be with beautiful lilac blossoms in the garden,
And Adam's timeless fears of Woman—of Pandora's box—
Proved providence untrue.

Early Morning, Wake Up Call!

Another chai awakens her to breathless
sensations,
Two lights flicker and flash into sleepy eyes,
Eight days of work to go,
Then, another job hunt,
Conveniently priced face paint to make-up for aged
hand bags full of lipstick,
A trains sounds off,
As lightening clashes the sunlight,
The auto spits out fumes into the cold morning
All make a run for it
Off to school
Off to rule
If only the market had been true
Maybe she wouldn't have stuck like glue

A Daughter

A girl takes her place in the family tree
Her mother's role as a model prevails
A girl respects parents dutifully
In turn, they confirm her ancient fairy tales

Stories that teach how to relate to peers
Mom knows all too soon she will be grown up
That mom responds to all her daughter tears and
cheers
Ensuring always she holds a full cup

Too soon, she will travel afar, alone,
And forgo her mother's heartfelt advice
When all the world's for her to rule and own
If she tries not once but also thrice

If you, my daughter, do live joyfully
It's in your hands to prevail triumphantly.

Do not take these poems seriously
But interpret them as be fit to thee.

The following pages deal with the writing process
in the college or high school classroom.

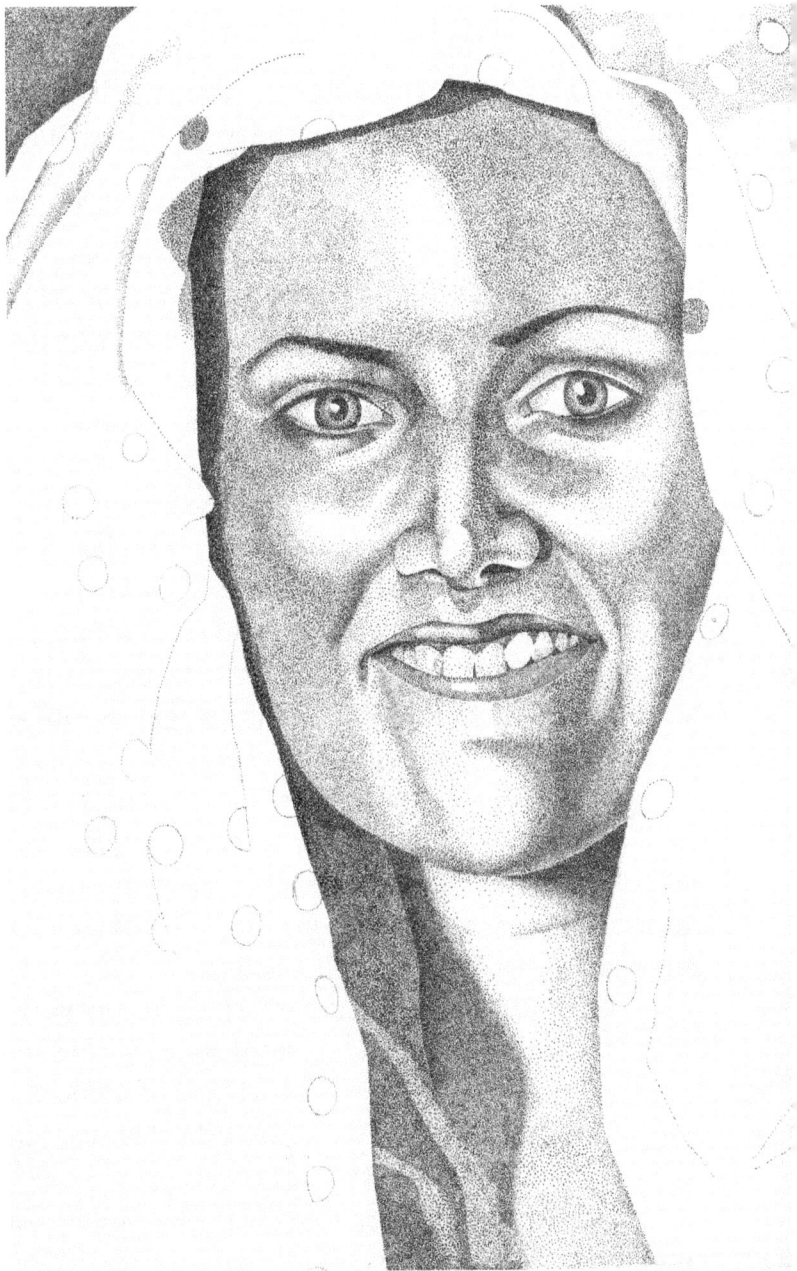

1983 Self-portrait

The Best Approach to Writing Instruction:
Integrating Creativity with Mechanics

It is imperative that a writing pedagogy address the creative aspects of writing along with the basics of composition. This association is absolutely necessary since authors must learn to fuse the spontaneous characteristics of creative writing with technical, formal writing structures. Simply put, students must be prepared to construct eloquent and well-organized essays that are easily understood, original, and fun to read. Teachers facilitate an understanding among their students that it is both desirable and even acceptable to challenge the writing paradigm and traditional ideology—once the students have mastered the laws of mechanics. This combination of fluidity and traditional structure is the essence that enables the great voices in literature.

The teacher's role is henceforth that of a facilitator in the discovery of a unique and effective voice. There is a great deal of literature that supports the assertion that teachers empower students through writing. According to Haake, author of <u>What Our Speech Disrupts</u>,

> Our purpose as creative writing teachers ought to be to construct a nonhierarchical space within which we can expand prior notions of what might count as writing and extend to every student the privilege of his or her own speech. (18-19)

Without the ability to express themselves successfully, emergent writers cannot affect change or represent their native cultures successfully. Lower-level learners remain voiceless, which is why past societies failed to give certain ethnicities, and the female gender, the opportunity to discover the full range of opportunities in reading and writing. Today, however, the creative writing teacher is a key player in the development of a personal voice and the acquisition of culture.

Haake urges readers to re-examine the purpose of creative writing studies, and to consider that writing enables students to better understand their own essence.

On the whole, this book (<u>What Our Speech Disrupts</u>) argues for a shift within the discipline that would respond to student differences and allow for conceiving creative writing as a practice that takes many forms of value in the lives and educations of our students.

This practice is open-ended in that it is accepting of all genders, ethnicities and viewpoints. According to Haake,

Such a classroom might be conceived of as a site of bricolage, where the teacher-writer, together with her or his student-writers, uses everything at hand not just to make writing happen, but to do so within a critical framework that reveals writing systems and gives students authority over their own work. (18)

If students are to develop a voice, they must be empowered through knowledge of the mechanics and creative techniques behind the structure. No matter how meaningful their statements may be, the students' intent must be clearly understood by others. Authors who acknowledge the need to develop a voice express as much concern about the structure of language as the approaches to expression. According to Selling, "One part of writing is to pick an interesting subject. However, the more important part is to develop techniques and skills that make the most ordinary subject interesting." (36)

The creative writing teacher must be able to assist students in developing rudimentary mechanics along with basic skills to organize their ideas effectively. To be more specific, some of these techniques may include graphic organizers, sketches, outlines, and chronological tables. The organization of the paragraph must follow logical rules as it moves from topic sentence to the supporting details and conclusion;

meanwhile, a natural flow must occur as one paragraph leads to the next, and each must maintain appropriate topics as well as a logical order.

Beginning students can best organize ideas and grasp the structure of writing if it is based upon their own lives. Selling encourages teachers to adapt life story writing to help students increase technique and voice.

> This writing approach is intended and has been used to give students the opportunity to develop a command of the language as a mode of communication. Within this developing language, it is appropriate for young people to see that having feelings, knowing what those feelings are, and expressing them on paper are entirely normal parts of ordinary life experience. (41)

A writing curriculum that, in some manner, engages students in the act of recreating moments from personal recollection may lead to many other possibilities for self-expression, such as fiction based on personal memories, creative nonfiction, and poetry. Therefore, as an intrinsic part of today's pedagogy, the author would insist upon integrating the personal memoir in all undergraduate or secondary school creative writing curriculums.

Without doubt, there is a sense of hesitancy when assigning writing based upon students' personal experiences since teachers generally fear entry into unknown and unfamiliar rooms. It is essential to remember that writers are the ones who have the courage to encounter that which others fear, and to ask the questions others dare not pose. This is precisely how a writer acquires her individual voice.

A voice, the essence of life, will not be powerful if it does not integrate the creative aspects of writing with its logical and structural mechanics. One of the best techniques to develop structure and mechanics is that of turning to the narrative masters or reviewing the works most admired by students. This could include master narratives in children's literature. Sims writes,

> If you ask most writers how they learned to write, as I
> have the ones who appear in this anthology, they will
> tell you it was by reading the works of men and women
> who were doing the kind of writing they want to do and
> trying to figure out how they did it. (1)

The implications of this are that a sound pedagogy
integrates examples of quality writing that appeal to student
writers. For example, the author is about to read five memoirs
prior to her attempt at writing her own. In order to target the
manuscript to a particular market, it is important that she get a
feel for the style of a few successful authors who have written
within the same genre. Such teaching and learning techniques
used by professionals are applicable to students at all levels.

Oates, the editor of Telling Stories, suggests teachers
should integrate the miniature narratives into their lessons as
models for later writing:

> 'Miniature' narratives come first for obvious reasons:
> like the dramatic monologue (to follow), they present
> beginning writers with a form far more accessible and
> navigable than the traditional story of greater length and
> complexity. (3)

Ramjerdi gives credit to master narratives for being the basis
for all stories that are to be created: "I would argue that
virtually all works that are read in fiction workshops now are at
the same time repetitions of antithesis of gradations of a
master narrative." (Ramjerdi and Garber 18-19) Whether or
not teachers agree with Ramjerdi's premise, no one denies that
master narratives provide an excellent model to either emulate
or contrast. Among other important factors, master narratives
exemplify solid grammatical structure along with stimulation
for creative ideas.

Students should be encouraged to absorb ideas and
structures from the master narratives of other cultures. As an
exercise in writing, students who are bilingual may get extra

credit for translating texts from foreign writers. When students have studied the professionals or the masters from various multicultural genres, they will have moved closer to acquiring a mature and effective technique. This study of masters is an essential step that all writers must take, whether it is within the framework of the Sweeney Pedagogy Class, or at some point in the students' journey to personal mastery.

Perhaps the most significant aspect of the master narrative is the logical flow of events that enables readers to understand the text. The progression is typically from the development of a problem (conflict) to a climax, followed by a resolution. Teachers must challenge their students with these problems by assigning short fictional writing assignments similar to the miniature narratives they have studied. In making the assignment, the students will be asked to address problems that one might encounter on a daily basis, and craft individualized resolutions. The ultimate resolution, although definitive, should leave room for thought afterward.

Master narratives make one's life easier as a teacher because they provide writing instructors with high quality stories that are eminently suitable for discussion. Students readily accept the value offered by time-tested master narratives. Indeed, these archetypal models are handed down from one generation to the next as ancestral gifts that provide a sense of history and interconnectedness. It is this feeling of continuity that teachers must establish in the writing classroom through critique and mentorship. According to Johanna Hurwitz,

> I was fortunate to always be surrounded by books and people who read...Both my parents and my grandmother read to me and I vividly remember enjoying the public library that was just a short walk from our apartment.

Luckily, Hurwitz was exposed to master narratives as well as relatives who served as her writing mentors. (Koehler-

Pentacoff 271)

Student writers may not realize that most writers have benefited to varying degrees from the assistance of a mentor as they developed their writing voice. This may be one of the best-kept secrets in writing instruction: Students need individuals who will give them encouragement and whom they can emulate. Effective mentoring is a critical element within the pedagogy that is enhanced when teachers match mentoring pairs who are assigned to give one another encouragement and advice.

In my class, each student will have a mentoring partner with whom he or she will discuss writing topics. Mentoring partners support one another by providing valuable, targeted and affable counsel regarding the improvement of each other's work. They can discuss readings, edit one another's work, and share their findings with others in the group. It is likely most students will want a mentoring partner and will gladly accept the teacher's assignment thereof. Students enjoy caring feedback provided in safe and personal environments, but they are often too hesitant to seek criticism on their own. There are many excellent examples of mentoring partnerships in the English-to-speakers-of-other-languages classrooms in which peers review one another's work and jointly assist in the editing and revision processes.

Selling has written a chapter on the importance of giving feedback to fellow students. He urges teachers to engage students in the critique process since giving and receiving feedback from mentors can be as meaningful as the writing process itself. He says that "It is possible, however, to form groups within classrooms that have entirely different dynamics." Demonstrably, these are the groups in which student writers can feel at ease. In smaller groups, "The writer does not feel it necessary to defend his or her work and can, instead, focus on understanding how others are receiving it."(52-53) The writing class, therefore, is all about developing this sense of community.

Students will learn more about one another, and about writing, through the establishment of a friendly learning community within the larger framework of the classroom. This is one reason why the author has integrated computer-art and computer-writing critiques for students. Such practices, formerly regarded as strategies for teaching lower-level learners, have become increasingly important in a technology-based, visual world. Classroom critiques nowadays must be integrated with Internet communications in the form of message boards. This medium is currently an integral part of the writing process, and it has proven attractive to writers with diverse learning styles.

Anyone who has taught students that possess a wide range of abilities, learning styles, and talents understands well that teachers should never assume learners *know* the material. The writing instructor must question students in order to ascertain whether they truly comprehend what is expected of them. The teacher must specifically address issues regarding grammar, mechanics, and creative processes. In turn, questions posed by the students themselves indicate they are learning, and no question is too simple to be presented to the group. Indeed, it is the writer's job to pose such questions and seek answers relative to integrating mechanics and creativity.

Effective writing pedagogies strive to fuse spontaneous, creative production with a grammatically correct structure. Therefore, assignments combine mechanics with creativity to both establish balance and make a powerful statement concerning the development and use of student voices. Critiques, mentoring, and portfolio production represent efficient strategies that move students along the path toward achieving these goals.

Teachers should modify portions of the curriculum to meet the needs of diverse learners. Students benefit from exposure to a variety of genres including persuasive essays, poetry, and dialogue. Some of them will opt to specialize in specific genres since very few writers tend to drift toward analytical writing. Others are more spontaneous. Writing teachers can choose to advocate individual instruction while assisting students to learn useful techniques such as brainstorming, free association, and burrowing.

Burrowing is especially helpful for those students who absorb the world around them and dig deep into their souls. By its name alone, burrowing suggests excavating to the depths of consciousness with structure and great thought. In <u>What Our Speech Disrupts</u>, Haake says that burrowing is the use of ideas based upon a sentence. "Writing proceeds from language rather than image." (177-79) One sentence leads to the next. The process is akin to free association, except that it involves sentences that inspire successive sentences.

In contrast, free association is the challenge of writing as much as one can within a given amount of time while permitting one idea, rather than a sentence, to foment the next. This enables the writer to be as creative as possible, often pairing two concepts that are frequently antithetical. Free association also has much in common with brainstorming, itself generally a function of the prewriting process.

Brainstorming entails working on a team and surfacing ideas that might seem crazy to some, or even deriving solutions to problems. Mentoring partners may be asked to brainstorm new plots for fiction in a bid to be helpful to one another, much like a critique process. Whatever the assignment, however, one finds that working with others in the writing class builds teams.

Team building is an effective methodology that involves the establishment of multiple intelligence groups. On such teams, students pair with like-minded peers to brainstorm and edit texts. The Myers-Briggs Type Indicator personality questionnaire can be employed to assist in pairing those who have similar personality traits. These corresponding groups of students are very effective when discussing creative visualization techniques and reflections from life.

Teams and critique groups will encounter issues of ethnocentrism and the ethnocentric versus the multicultural voice. At present, these are two sizzling topics that follow the emergence of writers from all cultures whose work expands the context of the English-based writing world. Such topics fall within the realm of spontaneous and grammatical writing as they force classmates to find creative solutions to the gap between ethnocentrism and multiculturalism. It is interesting to examine how immigration and limited English proficiency affect the mechanics of the English language, and to what extent one can, or even should, deviate from normative writing models. A few authors have begun to integrate new word patterns into their texts such as *Spanglish*, a new *language* that has found its way into the mainstream from longstanding bilingualism.

Multiculturalism and diverse perspectives enhance creative writing. Indeed, eschewing conformity—daring to be different rather than *safe*—represents the very nature of the creative voice. Students' origins often become the seeds of triggering subjects; in other words, their various experiences serve as the inspiration for such students to become writers. Moreover, a triggering subject that arouses the desire to express one's passion is the very definition of a writer's motivation. The triggering subjects for some individuals motivate them to endeavor naturally in various arts, often because they have experienced difficulty or euphoria. Other students, however, require assistance in identifying a suitably catalytic triggering subject, the likes of which may be as radiant as "Princess Diana", as groundbreaking as The Beatles, or as gentle and fleeting as the memory of a kind deed. Triggering subjects are undeniably and extraordinarily personal, and they require acceptance within teams of students engaged in the critique process.

A writing pedagogy that integrates the creative and the mechanical aspects of language facilitates openness and candor in discussions. Suitably enabled minds inspire the emergence of new ideas, which is essentially the intent behind encouraging culturally diverse writers to express a personal voice. The teacher serves as a role model for the students as they observe the instructor's verbal and written responses to their products. Miller writes, "You should always be careful to treat both your audience and your opinions with respect. Few are likely to be converted to your opinions if you treat them like fools and dismiss their beliefs with contempt." (1-3) Only when students learn the mechanics of persuasive essays do they fully understand the necessity of treating opposing viewpoints with respect. As an analogy to life lessons, the student writers will learn that many points of view can be advanced or suitably defended if one adequately prepares her statements.

In conclusion to the new Pedagogy Integrating Creativity and Mechanics, the author wishes to provide a few practical suggestions for teaching that will provide outlets for imaginative expression. The following assignments deal with empathy, characterization, and protagonists.

In the first exercise, the students will interview someone who is of a different culture or age group. Their questions will surround the experience he or she identifies as having been the most effective learning experience over the years. The results of the interviews will be shared with the class. For the second exercise, the students will create a flawed character and explain the psychology that led to the character's distinctiveness. During the third assignment, the student writers will use index cards to create three protagonists for a fictional story dealing with opposing points of view. The students will later expand these ideas into stories and plays. Afterward, peer writers will trade work and edit each other's texts prior to commencing the final draft.

Teacher responses and evaluations are essential in providing instruction in creativity and writing mechanics. Above all else, evaluation is critical for creative writing students because it affirms their ability to take the steps necessary to improve their work. Evaluation includes summarizing the teacher's understanding of student efforts. The instructor must read student writers' works critically to achieve a full understanding of the overall meaning of that writing. Naturally, different teachers will rely on individual interpretations and understandings of student work, just as separate publishers have conflicting opinions about whether a particular manuscript is worthy of publishing. Since negative criticism from a teacher might inadvertently cause the end of a student's budding writing career, it is necessary to convey the logic that the instructor's opinions are merely subjective.

The best way to prevent grading from hindering creativity—or worse, making students abandon it altogether—is to grade multiple aspects of the writing. Teachers should pay attention separately to creative originality, analysis, and grammar and mechanics. There are many methods by which teachers can recognize compartmentalized abilities, either through separately grading creativity and mechanics or by providing students with a score for each. Regardless of whether college-level writing teachers establish such guidelines for grading, the instructor must be sensitive to these creative and mechanical components, individually and collectively, of effective writing.

Research in the area of creative writing instruction indicates there is a need for creative writing classes that focus strong emphasis on the analytical and intuitive aspects of writing. These are separate but unified forms of creativity and mechanics. Students must be encouraged to think independently while they develop a logical voice, which they reinforce with a solid foundation in both grammar and research.

In the real world, an artist employs technique and imagination to create a work of perceived genius. A musician adds masterful expression to the notes he has rigorously followed. Likewise, writing students persist in combining the spontaneous aspects of creativity with formal writing structures to ensure their melodic and emerging voices will be heard by all.

Works Cited

Daigh, Ralph. Maybe You Should Write a Book. Englewood

Cliffs: Prentice Hall, 1973.

Haake, Katherine. What Our Speech Disrupts. United States:

Premium Source Publishing, 2005.

Koehler-Pentacoff, Elizabeth. The ABCs of Writing for

Children. New York: Barnes and Noble, 2003.

Miller, Robert K. The Informed Argument: A Multidisciplinary

Reader and Guide. Orlando: Harcourt Brace Jovanich,

Inc., 1992.

Oates, Joyce Carol, ed. Telling Stories: An Anthology for

Writers. New York: W.W. Norton and Company, 1998.

Ramjerdi, Jan, and Eugene Garber. "Reflection on the

Teaching of Creative Writing." Colors of a Different

Horse (1994): 18-19.

Selling, Bernard. Writing Your Life Story: Using Life Stories to

<u>Develop Your Writing Skills</u>. 2nd ed. United States: Barnes and Noble, 1994.

Sims, Patsy, ed. <u>Literary Nonfiction: Learning by Example</u>. New York: Oxford U P, 2002. (Zinsser)

Zinsser, William. <u>On Writing Well</u>. 4th ed. New York: Harper Collins Publishers, 1990.

All photos of Ireland by Gael Sweeney